THE DOORBELLS *of* FLORENCE

the DOORBELLS of FLORENCE

fictional stories
and photographs

ANDREW LOSOWSKY

CHRONICLE BOOKS
SAN FRANCISCO

Library of Congress Cataloging-in-Publication Data:

Losowsky, Andrew, 1978–

    The Doorbells of Florence : stories / Andrew Losowsky.

      p. cm.

    ISBN 978-0-8118-6649-1

    1. Italians—Fiction. 2. Neighborhood—Fiction. 3. Doorbells—
Fiction. 4. Florence (Italy)—Fiction. I. Title.

PR6112.O76D66 2009

823'.92--dc22

2008022668

Manufactured in China

Cover and interior design by Andrew D. Schapiro

10 9 8 7 6 5 4 3 2 1

Chronicle Books LLC

680 Second Street

San Francisco, CA 94107

www.chroniclebooks.com

for LYRA

All stories are true,
and some of them actually happened.

ITALIAN PROVERB

Borgo Ognissanti, 23

She lives at number 5 and she doesn't exist.

She has no papers. If asked where she's from, she says, "Somewhere . . . to the east," in a vague voice, then changes the subject. She has no family, no history, no roots.

One day not long ago, as she walked slowly around the lake in Cascine Park, she thought again about how her life would be if she were allowed to exist. Maybe she'd be a fairy-tale princess, or the wife of someone very important. She would help him get out of bed and make him breakfast, kiss him on the lips, and watch him walk out the door of their expensive penthouse flat in Bana Jelacic Square.

She would then spend her days lying in turn on each of their five sofas, thinking about him and counting the hours until he returned. After lunch, she would sit on their balcony and look through her passport filled with smudged stamps, reminding herself of the exotic places they had been. In between the pages would be receipts from hotels where they had checked in together with real names, paid with real cheques and ordered room service that they didn't want but had ordered anyway because they could and it didn't matter.

Today, as she walks through the trees and tries to keep the damp leaves from staining her sheer stockings, she sees a man shuffling toward her. She keeps her eyes low, letting him watch her. And then she sees who it is and she stops and she waits. He approaches in his slow, deliberate manner, moving as if he lives in a body twenty years older than his face.

When she supposes that he is close enough to hear, she speaks quickly the Italian words she has practiced. "What is it you want? Should I save the money for you? Should we meet next time somewhere else? A hotel perhaps? Or . . ."

But the same thing happens as before. He stops, bows, and, gently taking her hand, places a two-euro coin into her palm before clasping her fingers around it. He smiles, nods, and then shuffles away in the direction he came.

"Thank you! Again!" she shouts after him but receives no acknowledgment.

He ignores the other girls, as he always does, and slowly becomes a silhouette, then a line, then a dot, then nothing. She places the coin in her bag. That night, she will add it to the jar containing the other two-euro coins he has given her.

She is afraid to spend them in case, one day, he asks her to do something terrible and she doesn't have the option to refuse. You never can tell, no matter how gentle they look.

When clients ask her name, she says, "Pichka." It is a rude word in her language and it amuses her to hear them say it.

Via dell' Ariento, 8

On the first day after he lost his job, Paolo Ringressi stayed in bed.

The second day, he crawled and stumbled around his flat, and drank milk. He didn't feel anything apart from unease at the change in his circumstances.

The third day, he mumbled words to no one in particular and ate soft food from a jar he found in the cupboard.

The fourth day, he created an imaginary friend, who saw him through days five to ten, when he ate whatever was left in his kitchen and read nothing but comic books.

Day eleven he left the house for the first time since it happened, bought a range of unhealthy products in brightly colored boxes, and started to think about girls.

Day twelve, he got spots.

Days thirteen to seventeen were mostly taken up with strange moods, spots, music, and masturbation.

Day eighteen, he finally cleaned himself up, went to a bar, and met some new people whom he wasn't sure whether or not he liked, but at least the change seemed positive. They suggested some books he might like to read. He spent days nineteen to twenty-one starting each one of them, and giving up soon after.

Day twenty-two, he went to some overpriced shops and bought himself some products he didn't need and would one day be able to afford.

Day twenty-six, he fell in love. Nothing much changed for two weeks.

On day forty, his love left him. He immediately went out and bought an unnecessary gadget.

On day fifty-five, he found himself staring at crowds of people, wondering why they were rushing around and where they were going.

On day sixty, he decided that the outside world was more than he could cope with, and spent the next week at home in his slippers, occasionally going into his small garden to fiddle with plant cuttings. He retreated into himself again.

Two weeks later, he ate soft food from another jar he found in the cupboard and then got back into bed.

Halfway through day seventy-eight, he was offered a new job. He accepted immediately, and woke up the next day feeling like a new man.

Hotel Peng is the only nudist hotel for the under-thirties in Southern Europe.

LARGO ALiNARi, thirty-one

Lungarno Soderini,

Every two weeks, a delivery company sends a messenger with a small package to an unmarked door that has two doorbells.

On each occasion, the messenger rings both bells, waits, knocks.

On each occasion, the messenger rings both bells, waits, knocks, and doesn't look up.

On each occasion, the messenger rings both bells, waits, knocks, and doesn't look up at the tall chimney.

On each occasion, the messenger rings both bells, waits, knocks, and doesn't look up at the tall chimney that has just released a small paper kite into the air. The kite floats along the breeze, carrying a tiny parcel high above the rooftops. At some point, the tugging of the kite forces open a corner of the parcel, and the entire thing unfolds in a couple of seconds, dropping its cargo on the buildings, streets, people below.

Sometimes it's feathers. Sometimes it's slips of paper containing lines from famous love poems. On one memorable day near the Pitti Palace, it rained marshmallows.

Meanwhile, on each occasion, the messenger who has rung both bells, waited, knocked, and not looked up, pushes a piece of paper marked "Undelivered" through the unmarked letterbox. He then returns to the depot, oblivious to the tiny, unusual cloud that he has just delivered into the city sky.

This has continued for the last eighteen months. The client, who paid up front, demanded that they return to the door once a fortnight until the small package had been signed for. The package remains undelivered.

8

Vicolo degli Adimari, 46

When the third flat was burgled, all the tenants in the building agreed that something had to be done. Every person in this elegant, exclusive block of flats is a millionaire several times over, and they had tried various expensive security measures, none of which had managed to outwit the intruders.

After consultations with the police and a number of neighbours' gatherings, it was decided that the building itself just looked too fancy. With its ornate door decoration and shiny brass doorbell, it screamed "money" and whispered ". . . for the taking."

So they decided on a change of tack. Though it pained them to do so, the ancient mahogany was replaced with a scuffed steel door. The lightbulb over the lintel was carefully smashed. And the shining bright doorbell was replaced by the cheapest they could find.

At first, they all placed their names in the same style, handwritten in ballpoint (they borrowed one from a delivery man) and slotted unevenly behind the plastic. But one day, Primo Grandi decided on a whim to make his look even worse, placing a cheap sticker over his name, to give it that "temporary" feel.

The others started to talk. Was this a more sensible tactic? Would he now be less prone to robbery? Even more galling, did he really think that he could do faux-cheap better than they could?

Since that day, the overly competitive, mostly bored residents have spent much of their time searching for increasingly nasty-looking ways of putting their names on the door. Solutions have ranged from old price tags peeled off shoeboxes to notes scribbled with their left hand and placed at such an angle as might blow away in a strong wind. Every morning, on leaving the building, each resident scrutinises the previous day's efforts by his or her neighbours and tries to imagine something worse. On Vicolo degli Adimari this year, reverse chic is very much in.

borgo san frediano, II

What Caprice Battistini loves more than anything is that thin-sliced moment when she tries to imagine his name. When eventually uncovered, it becomes a name that she can whisper, a secret they both know, a name that has none of the loaded charge of a real name (which is a name that only true loves and mothers can say correctly). He will be Dark Eyes.

"Hello, Dark Eyes," she will whisper tomorrow morning, naked under him, biting his nose, pushing gently with her feet against the tangled, sweat-moistened sheet draped around and between them. Then he will whisper something back, the flicker of panic visible in his eyes as he thinks quickly of a name he can offer in return, a new name that speaks of her essential being, and of her soul. The wrong word would instantly offend her, and their moment of intimacy would be lost.

"Hello, Sexy," he will probably offer up, kissing her lips in desire and relief.

Their naming ceremony complete, they will lapse again into quick pecks and long, slow, wet clinches.

She won't be his first Sexy, but that doesn't matter. She learned long ago that, for men, the naming ceremony was nothing but a brief obstacle to overcome in those early, fumbling days when every touch and every word has the dangerous possibility of being the wrong one. They would understand each other's bodies long before each other's words.

The moment of naming is the most delicious of challenges. She loves the sensation of finding the right adjective, one that will form a new idea deep inside her. Each partner has his own place in her head and heart; each can be summoned in an instant—merely mouthing a name brings his smell to her nostrils, his appearance before her eyes, reminds her how he made her feel and how he felt on top of her. Whenever she is alone, she might conjure one out of nothing with a quiet whisper.

Soft Touch. Freckle Cheek. Strongman. Big Lips. Funny Boy. Firey. Cuteass. Man Smell. Growl. Sharp Tooth. Nipple Boy. Giggle. And row upon row of Eyes—Big, Bright, Soft, Hard, Wide, Blue. Sparkle. And now Dark.

She looks down at the floor and smiles. She takes a sip of her drink, looks up and sees a tall, handsome man walking toward her, dressed in a smart grey suit.

"I'm sorry I'm late," he says with an easy smile.

"It's fine," she replies, and gazes into his large, dark eyes.

After four days, six pens, and two notepads, she is ready. Belinda Giordano has finally created a handwritten typeface perfect for a doorbell in the modern age. Bold, confident, easy to read and yet hardworking, it speaks of a strong stone building, comfortable and pleasant, yet always striving for success. Tonight, she will sleep peacefully for the first time since her arrival.

As one of Italy's leading (though currently unemployed) graphologists, she had felt uncomfortable at how Signora Bardini was demonstrating her insecurities on the doorstep, how Signor Rossi revealed his loneliness. The proclivity to infidelity of Signora Cambi-Bassi she could take or leave, but together, it was all too much. Each time Belinda walked through her new front door, the subconscious messages of her neighbours' handwriting nagged insistently in her ear. And she hadn't met a single one of them.

She had to act. After a week of living with the irritation, Belinda marched out to the stationery shop and bought a

selection of pens of varying colours and thicknesses. A long and drawn-out process of experimentation was to follow. Four days later, supposing that her neighbours are out, Belinda has just removed the existing scrawls from behind the strips of plastic and slotted in her finely crafted replacements. She is about to return to her flat with their scraps of paper, where she will burn them in the fireplace.

She doesn't know what the other named parties will think about her actions—or if they will even notice. Few people, she knows, have such sensitivity to these matters. She doesn't really care, for finally she can enter her own house with a sense of pride.

Belinda will hold her first dinner party this weekend. She can't wait to hear what her friends will say when they cross the threshold.

Via Canto

Luigi likes it old school.

de' Nelli, 19

When she arrived in the city, Jemima Elliott felt very lost. Fortunately, the first thing she saw in her new flat was a map on the dining table.

Unfortunately, it was labeled in Cyrillic. But what better opportunity, thought she, to learn a new skill while discovering the city?

Even more unfortunately, Jemima was unable to decipher that it was actually a map of Bratislava. The circle in ballpoint, which she supposed marked the position of the flat, was in fact a rendezvous point for a clandestine exchange of packages.

As she explored her new neighbourhood, Jemima began to make connections between the strange lettering on the map and the Italian street names. Over a period of six weeks, she got herself hopelessly lost an average of three times a day— but she was not, she would always readily admit, very good with maps.

Slowly, however, she succeeded in superimposing Florentine buildings, streets, bridges, and landmarks onto the plan of the Slovak city. The Danube River became the Arno. St Martin's Cathedral was converted, on paper at least, into the Duomo. Very occasionally she would make small corrections, surprised at how dramatically construction must have overtaken cartography.

By the time she had been in Florence two months, the reality of one city had been perfectly placed on top of the other. She had also deciphered, erroneously, the entire Cyrillic alphabet.

One day, twelve weeks after her arrival, Jemima was a ten-minute walk from her flat when she realised she had forgotten her exotic map. She was about to turn and walk back home when she remembered that, the previous day and without a word of explanation, a strange man had shuffled up to her and given her a two-euro coin.

Jemima decided to go to a nearby kiosk and spend the money on a new map of Florence. She became so distressed by her new purchase that it took three and a half hours to find her way back to the flat.

Via Nazionale, 38

Every evening except Tuesdays, the Society for the Promotion of Deceased Italian Artists meets in these rooms for a series of parallel séances. On a good day, they may even channel a pencil sketch.

The works are then made available for sale or viewing in the back room of a nearby private gallery. "You have to understand the strains that the afterlife puts on their usual style," says Michele Barossi, gallery owner and chief channeler of Botticelli. All the sketches are still available, and prices start at 1.5 million euros.

borgo san Frediano, 1

"That's it," thought Emilio. "I'm going to be a detective." He was eight years old and had just read the entire series of Philip Marlowe books in a weekend. That afternoon, he cut holes in his father's newspaper and stared through them at passersby. He then practised leaving dead-letter drops under park benches for others to find, and every Saturday afternoon, he would quietly follow people he'd never met, noting down their movements in his notepad.

The older Emilio got, the more of an obsession it became. He left school at eighteen to turn pro. He hired a small room, put "L'Investigativa" on the doorbell, placed an ad in the local newspaper ("Experienced private detective. No case too big.

No case too small, either. Call Emilio. All cases accepted.") and waited for the work to come in.

The problem was that, since the age of eight, it wasn't just his ambition that had been growing. By the time he turned seventeen, Emilio had flat feet, a dandelion of bright red hair, and was six feet, five inches tall. In short, he was probably the clumsiest and most conspicuous private detective there has ever been. He also wasn't very good at it.

He had failed to discover if Signora Castifiore's husband was cheating on her and couldn't spot the waiters who pickpocketed at Signor Mostelli's restaurant. The would-be arsonist had left the scene long before Emilio had clomped his way down the street and peered in the shop window, while the Bagrone family's teenage daughter had spotted him straightaway and managed to give him the slip as soon as she had turned the first corner outside her school.

Within a month, the phone had stopped ringing. Emilio became thoroughly depressed. A kindly uncle felt sorry for his nephew and gave Emilio a job that he had already privately discarded as impossible—to find proof that one of his debtors, who claimed poverty, had a hidden private income.

Three of Florence's biggest debt-collection agencies had failed him. The uncle had written off the large sum and didn't begrudge adding a smaller sum to it if it would make his nephew feel better about things.

Emilio happily wrapped himself up in the task. He resolved not to return home until he had found the evidence he needed. The next morning he began, following the debtor everywhere he went, hiding behind corners, quietly noting his movements, watching carefully from a distance whenever he entered offices, shops, cafeterias, or bars. He did the whole thing by the book.

Which is why, two days later, a rush of blood sprang into Emilio's cheeks when the target turned around and began to approach him. He quickly changed direction, walked away, was about to cross the street when the man grabbed him by the arm. He seemed upset. "Will you please stop following me?" asked the target. "Look, I know you're there, I can guess who you're working for, and you're starting to freak me out."

Emilio stared at the ground and didn't reply. But he didn't give up either. He continued to sit in his car within sight of the man's house and slept there uncomfortably every night. Every time the target entered a building, Emilio would loiter in dark unseen corners in the vestibule, quietly rereading his Philip Marlowe books from front to back. He kept his distance, watching the entrances of offices, shops, cafeterias, bars.

The days passed slowly, but Emilio didn't mind. In truth, he wasn't sure what evidence he would find, as, unlike his hero, he was far too timid to attempt any investigation that might involve illegal entry or rifling through dustbins. As long as he was still on the case, that was surely enough. Patience, he felt, would eventually bring its rewards.

A week later, his uncle came to find him. The target was leaving a roadside cafeteria, while Emilio leaned on a wall across the street. He folded away his newspaper and was about to follow the man when his uncle came up behind him suddenly and grabbed his arm. The target was walking away at some speed. Emilio tried to shake off his employer, moving to follow the target.

"You don't understand. You don't have to do this anymore," said the uncle.

"No, you don't understand," replied Emilio. "I'm not going to mess this one up. I'm here until I find something." He started to leave, his eyes firmly on the small figure disappearing into the city crowds.

His uncle pulled him back. "No. You don't understand. You don't have to do this anymore because he paid up in full. In the bank, this morning. I have the money. He said that you're starting to scare him, and that people have begun to talk. They are laughing at how you are always there, wherever he goes. They'd even started to call you his boyfriend. He paid in cash—with interest, too—and made me promise that you'll never follow him again. That's a remarkable talent you have, Emilio. Congratulations. You cracked the case."

He'd remember that moment for the rest of his life. Those four words. Those magical four words.

Instantly, he realised what he would have to do. Instead of trying to be subtle, he would stand out. Instead of hiding in dark corners, he would place himself in broad daylight. Away with the dark suits and the raincoat. That afternoon, he spent half of his uncle's reward money in a costume shop. He tried on clown suits and bear costumes. He experimented with a nun's habit and the sharp silver edges of a robot. He felt them all a little too frivolous for the task, and settled instead on a long dark tailcoat and an unusually tall top hat. He became, from that day on, the Undertaker of Debt.

Now Emilio has five employees in the city, all unusually tall or short, clumsy but persistent, and with unforgettable faces. Their clients are always creditors, people frustrated with a slow, unfathomable, and occasionally corrupt Italian legal system, and who remain squeamish of hired thugs. Instead, they send in the Undertakers. Everyone in Florence now knows them and what they represent—a smart hat and tails marching down the street, faces powdered white with dark false shadows under their eyes, a large euro sign sewn onto the back of their coat. People point and laugh at the outfits and then look two meters ahead to see who the scarlet-faced debtor is, usually hurrying with head lowered, trying to lose their constant stalkers.

From work to restaurant, cinema to country picnic, the tail-coated shame follows these people everywhere, its strange shadow cast across their lives until they eventually pay up.

Emilio's company is about to open new offices in Rome and Milan. The work is so regular that he has trouble finding enough conspicuous people to take it all on. Best of all, his new company's success rate is 100 percent. Not even Philip Marlowe could boast that.

VIA dELL' ALBERO, 39

She finally left him on their anniversary. It was three years after their marriage and exactly eight years since the day they'd first met, which happened to be both his birthday and Christmas Day. It was a particularly miserable festive season for Fidelio.

Since that particular Yuletide, he has refused to acknowledge the existence of public holidays. He ignores other people's decorations and never wishes anyone a "Happy" anything. At work, he signs up for the holiday shifts that no one else wants and pretends that nothing unusual is going on. Epiphany, Easter, Liberation Day, Assumption are all salt poured onto his wounded heart.

But a man cannot work without rest. And so, after a long evening spent reading through his old diaries, Fidelio has invented a selection of personal celebrations that will allow him to take time off each year and that have no public relevance whatsoever.

She may have ruined his birthday and Christmas, he says to himself, but she'll never get close to Rainy Thursday, Finished That Book Day, or the Day of the Smart New Shoes.

via dei Martelli 72

There are more than thirty doorbells at the Raven Club. You ring one and then wait. If you're lucky and there's space, they'll buzz you in.

By the time you've walked down the black iron spiral stairs to the gentle strains of lounge jazz, the drink you rang for is waiting on the bar, freshly mixed by a genial artisan who is known only as Joe.

Via dei Gori,

Almost every night when she gets home, Camila sighs about "the boss" at "the lab." She never goes into more detail. Then she closes her eyes and enters a scared, empty silence.

At this point, Gino hugs her and says nothing. But each time this happens, the itch of Gino's curiosity spreads farther. It began as a tingle in the nape of his neck, scratched away in a moment. Then it twitched his right eyebrow for a full minute and a half. The next day, it moved to the back of his left hand and also ran along the fourth rib on his right side, twisting its way through nerves into his right ankle. Nothing, from hot baths to pharmaceuticals and vigorous scratching, would make it go away.

From her expression, Gino knows that he can never ask Camila about what is troubling her. Every time the shadow crosses her face, she sighs, shivers, and says nothing. When they go to bed, Gino holds her tight, and eventually, mercifully, she falls asleep. Meanwhile the curiosity, as if a malevolent worm, continues to burrow deeper into his skin. He tries to distract himself, thinking about football, about his family, about his work. But in those foggy moments just before falling asleep, the dark depths of his curiosity return.

Red parallel tramlines run across his body, plowed into his skin by the rough edges of his bitten fingernails. The lines cover his neck, his torso, and down the length of his right leg. When she asked him about it one day, he lied and told her it was eczema. She accepted the reply in silence and returned to the distant dark corner of her thoughts. Fearing for his sanity and his appearance, Gino now wears mittens to bed.

30

Via Delle Terme, Forty-Eight

Everyone stayed quiet except the rooster. At least, that's the way the story has been told to generations of Florentines, explaining how the attempted ambush on neighbouring Pisa, on September 21, 1406, failed. The rooster crowed, and so the position of the Florentine army was discovered.

It took another century, and the skills of Niccolò Machiavelli, before Pisa was eventually taken. That 1509 victory, however, gets far less attention in the history books than the defeat. The near-miss somehow epitomises the local spirit more than any victory could, and it has been commemorated by the city many times—by the Tuscan wine label Gallo Nero (Black Rooster), by nicknaming a particularly unpatriotic suburb of the city "Galluzzo," by banning such birds from being kept within the city walls between the years 1680 and 1922. Throughout Florence, the rooster has become a symbol of bad luck and of defeat.

It is in this tradition that a few patriotic Florentines gather each year at Beppe Rancoli's house. Numbers vary—in periods of bad fortune for the football club Fiorentina, as many as fifty people may come along. The early start combined with the violent finish, however, means an average attendance of around twenty.

They no longer use a real rooster—a wooden one is specially carved—but they enact the same ritual as people here have for longer than they can remember: beginning at

midnight on September 21, the group stands in front of the wooden rooster and implores it to be quiet. Poems are read, short scenes performed, long epics and allegorical stories are offered concerning the joys of silence, patriotism, and the victory that could have been. They beg, threaten, and sweet-talk the wooden bird not to crow. It never responds.

At dawn, their efforts exhausted, the group then carries the rooster to a nearby hilltop overlooking the city and shoots it for treason. Its splinters scatter across the grass, joining those of previous roosters. Honor satisfied, the group returns to the city and their normal lives for another year—during which idle moments are spent preparing for the following year's literary marksmanship.

If you watch carefully, you'll see that most Florentines still flinch when they hear a cock crow.

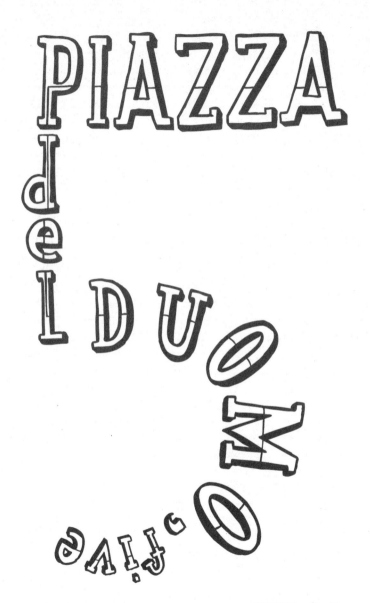

PIAZZA del DUOMO, five

After he bought the building, Bernardo Salterini (known in his day as "Il Magnifico") had to fight for more than three years for the necessary planning permission to convert it into his dream house. What he wanted was simple: to obliterate three of the four levels in the six-hundred-year-old building, leaving only the attic intact. It took relatives on the council and an imaginative local mayor to make it possible.

It then took another year and nine months before the work was finished, with Florence's oldest construction company, Il Amico di Calzolaio (founded: 1509), devoting half of its man-hours and several subcontractors to the project.

On the day it was finished, Bernardo answered the telephone in his rented flat, let out a whoop, immediately opened the front door, and started to run the two kilometers to the door where Giuseppe Caglieri, twenty-nine-times-great grandson of the construction company's founder, was smiling behind his enormous moustache and holding in his large hand the key.

Bernardo arrived, panting, eight minutes and eighteen seconds after setting off. He grabbed the key from Giuseppe and opened the door. It was more beautiful than he could have imagined. To Giuseppe, it looked like the work of a giant spider that had perhaps been experimenting with hard drugs. However, he had completed it exactly to order, and he couldn't help but feel professional pride overwhelm his personal tastes.

Bernardo stepped inside and looked up. The light fell slowly from the front and back windows on the third floor— all of the other windows were bricked shut. A tangle of ropes hung from the walls and the high, high ceiling. At various points, they twisted and weaved together, then split apart just as suddenly, stretching out to the walls and roof, where they were secured by heavy metal brackets. The arrangement seemed random, without the symmetry or mathematics of a spider's rose. The precision of re-creating something that seemed so imprecise had nearly beaten Giuseppe. But in the end, the shaky sketch on the back of a telephone bill, which Bernardo insisted was the perfect reproduction of a dream he had had one inspired night, had been realised, right down to the tiniest of details.

In another story, Bernardo would perhaps have fallen into a radioactive vat of bubbling liquid and emerged a supervillain. In this one, however, he is someone who retired five years ago from the circus ring, only to find that after so many years hanging from a trapeze, living on the ground gave him vertigo. Only when suspended from a great height, away from the dangers of the average home (where 90 percent of accidents happen, he reminds people constantly), does he ever feel safe.

He lives here still. His bed and amenities are on the top floor, surrounding a large hole in the floor that lets him fall directly onto the ropes. He has positioned a television where once was a second-floor showerhead. He has created his own intricate nets of string and twine between the huge ropes, now favorite spots for reading and eating. When not in the normal-looking attic, his exists in perpetual suspension. Bernardo freely admits to visitors that they will most likely hate the inconvenience of his unusual living space. Their children, however, always love it.

Via Jei Martelli, 11

"We hope that you've enjoyed your flight with us today. For those of you holidaying here for the first time, don't forget to visit the awe-inspiring Duomo church, the jewelry shops on the glittering Ponte Vecchio, and of course the manly figure of Michelangelo's *David*, before you enjoy a lovely pizza in a piazza. Just some of the essential sights here in glorious Florence."

Except he's never seen them. Not one of them. He finishes reading out the words, switches off the cabin microphone, and sighs. He closes his eyes for a moment, leaning back in his chair at the front of the plane as the passengers wait for the flight attendant to unlock the door. He takes a breath and prepares himself for the same airport small talk as the crew walks through passport control, on his way to the same airline-owned, one-person flat, with its slightly mocking code name taped on the door. He takes another breath and thinks about the rest of his evening.

He will sit for a moment on the as-new soft furnishings before rising to brush his teeth with sour Italian toothpaste. He will shower, change from his uniform into one of the three identical pairs of Gap jeans and Gap T-shirts he has in his regulation-size hand baggage, then walk to the bar on the corner. He will order the same ham and cheese panini washed down with the same order of Coca-Cola (no ice), stare at the same flickering television screen shouting a language he doesn't understand, ignore the same clientele (or people just like them), walk back to the flat, and go to bed at the same hour (more or less) as last time, and the time before that.

He never feels that he's in Florence, just as he never felt yesterday that he was in Barcelona, last week in Paris, last month in Stockholm, in Berlin. Away from home, he lives in transit, a land inhabited by shapes and noises that drift around him like wisps of cloud. On their return to the plane, other crew members will talk of places, exploits, sights, sites. He will nod, smile, and then return to this cockpit, or one identical to it.

In the coming days and weeks, as he returns again and again to the most romantic and evocative cities in Europe, he will continue to read the same paragraphs aloud over the microphone, but he will never once stop to think about what the words mean. He is afraid that, if he sees just one of the incredible sights hinted at in the prepared script, he might want to stay forever in any one of the places that he passes through. And that would ruin everything.

BORGO LA NOCE, 28

When Enzo said he was moving out, Federico was furious. It had all been so perfect. He had spent months looking for a building where the occupants, like his record collection, his books, his wall posters, his wardrobe, and his refrigerator, were arranged in alphabetical order.

When Bernardo moved out of the attic, he had begged his cousin Donnie to move in. When his cousin had finally relented (Federico currently pays a third of Donnie's rent on top of his own), it was even better. Alphabetical. In sequence. Amazing.

Then Enzo had to go and spoil it all by wanting to move in with his girlfriend in Pisa. Each time that the landlord had brought a prospective new tenant into the building, Federico had made sure that he was around, lurking on the stairs, introducing himself loudly and listening hopefully to the names offered in reply. Gianluca Vespasiani, Alisia Montagna, Cara Genco, and Victor Alinari were so, so wrong. He muttered "rising damp" in Luca's ear, hissed "rat droppings" at Cara. They couldn't move in. It wasn't right. It would ruin everything.

But one fateful day, one hideous, awful day, Federico happened to be away in the hills, walking with his uncle. In his absence, Luciano—Lucci to pretty much everyone—had come to the flat, liked it, and within a week had moved in. Federico nearly had a screaming fit. Luckily, thankfully, wonderfully, it turns out that his surname is Eranio. But the mean-spirited Lucci refuses to put it on the bell.

"No one will know it's me," he shrugs, offering "Lucci Eranio" as a useless compromise.

Right now, Federico is being extra nice, popping round with "leftovers," cleaning Lucci's bike, repainting his skirting boards. Lucci doesn't mind any of that. Federico is just waiting for the day that Lucci relents and puts only his surname on the bell. Unfortunately, he won't.

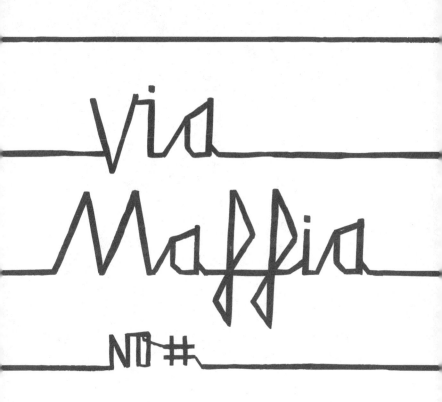

Ever since 1509, it has been illegal for this door to have any form of bell, knocker, handle, or keyhole. The couple that lives here today pays only one euro a year for rent—but one of them always has to stay in.

via di Santo Spirito, 4

One day last week, a girl called Cira, who was visiting her boyfriend in this building, accidentally pressed the wrong bell.

She realised her mistake straight away, but the voice that replied was so warm and unexpected that something compelled her to keep talking. Within five minutes, she had told the voice about the situation with her family, the boyfriend she wasn't sure she loved, and why she was struggling in her studies and had started to explain how her cat no longer liked being tickled behind the ears, and did he have any idea what this might mean about their relationship?

The voice listened and answered, calmly and wisely. Each time it spoke, she felt a shiver in her chest that wouldn't go away. She stood there for so long, and was so late for her date, that her boyfriend became convinced that something awful must have happened.

Eventually, having called her house and received no answer, he walked down the stairs and was surprised to find Cira outside his front door, talking to someone through the grille. He took her arm firmly and suggested that they walk to the local bar for a coffee. She refused, pushing him to one side, returning to apologize to the voice for the interruption. Confused, her boyfriend tried again, pulling her arm harder still. She pushed him once more.

Things escalated from there. The kerfuffle had gathered quite a crowd, and soon a passing policeman was called upon to break it up. A local reporter, who lived nearby and was watching the whole thing first from his balcony and then from his doorstep, ventured to speak into the grille to find out what had happened.

"I have no idea," came the rich, warm reply. The young man stammered another question back. As the crowd dispersed, he stayed on the doorstep, talking, discussing, sharing stories with the humane, witty, deep voice on the other end.

After nearly two hours of conversation, he realised that he was so late for work that he may have to make a choice between his job and the voice. He found that it was physically painful to walk away—he had been in the same position for so long, his legs had cramped stiff. Career ambition had eventually forced him into action, but deep down, he knew that he had made the wrong decision.

As his legs wobbled and carried him uneasily away, he saw a waitress from the café across the road start to move toward the anonymous doorway. The reporter felt a long snake of jealousy uncurl itself in his heart and he looked away quickly. As a result, he nearly walked into a small man who was also struggling to control his legs. He stammered an apology, but the unsteady man only winked and slipped a large round coin into his hand.

In total, eleven women, three men, and a stray Labrador spent time at the grille that day, fascinated by the untiring voice that spoke only to them from somewhere inside the small building.

And then, in the middle of Rocio's explanation of how complicated her aunt's inheritance would be to distribute, the sound cut out. The bell had stopped working. As no one knew for sure which flat the voice had come from, no one dared go inside and plead for its owner to continue.

Some say that the voice melted the circuitry. Others, who weren't privy to its power, wonder if the voice existed at all. For all those who sat on the hard concrete doorstep that strange, wonderful day, it is now little more than a comforting memory.

But not for Domani Bertocci. She lives in the building, and for much of the duration of the voice's spell, she was sitting in her flat, listening in on the internal telephone, hearing people share their stories with a voice that came from somewhere close by. She hadn't dared to say a word. Finally, her envy, her frustration, and her fear had cut so deeply into her that she had gone downstairs with a pair of scissors and sliced the thin electric wires leading to the doorbell. She has been crying herself to sleep every night since.

Via della Scalla, 7

Her moment came in 1984. Until then, Donata Topini had
been born at the wrong time for her ideas. At school, she had
come up with a simple modification that would have made
the spinning jenny twice as efficient. At the university, she
invented a padded laptop bag that folded into a table—nearly
twenty years before the laptop existed. (By the time it did, she
had forgotten the details of her creation.) Her genius seemed
forever cursed by anachronism.

But then, one summer's day in 1984, she had the perfect
idea at the perfect moment. The revelation came to her as she
left her friend Fabiola's stationery shop. They had just been
marveling at what had arrived by mistake from an American
supplier: boxes and boxes of greeting cards for pointless
holidays. Hundreds of meaningless pieces of paper filled with
vacuous poetry that no one would ever read. Valentine's Day

she knew, but what was Grandparents' Day? And who sends cards for Halloween?

She left the shop, mounted her bicycle, and pondered the whole affair as she rode home. What was the point of all this paper? Who was spending time and money exchanging things on made-up holidays? And if they are going to invent a new holiday, why not create something useful?

She nearly crashed her bicycle. She stopped at the side of the road, reached for the notepad in her back pocket, and half-assaulted the nearest passerby in the hunt for a pen.

The idea was refined and then discussed at length with her friends, one of whom wrote about it in his "This Crazy Town" column of the local newspaper that week, which was read by the mayor's wife, who passed it to her husband to read over breakfast on the very day that he was expected at the provincial meeting of business entrepreneurs and was nervous that he had, as yet, come up with no good ideas that would show him to be the forward-thinker that he had claimed to be during the campaign. He read the story over, twice. He waved his wife away and read it a third time while pouring coffee into his cup, not noticing that the cup was already full and the coffee was now flowing over its rim and onto the floor in a steady stream.

That afternoon, he called Donata into his office, where he invited her to sign a document and they agreed on a consultancy fee. An hour later, he announced it to the local and national media: October 15, 1984, would be Florence's first "Il Giorno di Contatti"—Contacts Day.

Instead of greeting cards, everyone would give out business cards—but not their own. Instead, they would carefully choose another contact from those they already had who would prove useful to the recipient, and pass it on, each year on this day; and so the ability to network on others' behalf would become both a sign of people's connectedness and a demonstration of how much they valued precious friends and clients.

It was the perfect solution for a faltering economy. Address books would grow fatter, and local businesses would move closer together. Useful information in every sector would slowly be dispersed through the city. "I got your card on Contacts Day," would begin speculative telephone calls. (To caution against abuse, a city edict swiftly banned telemarketers.)

In its first year, people were skeptical, and only a few office comedians participated. Within two years, however, business leaders and lowly workers alike could be found, a week before the event, frantically handing out their business cards in the hope of picking up new contacts later; others would leave piles of their cards on park benches or in swimming pool changing rooms. Businesses showed off their popularity with strings of other people's cards as window dressing. In many houses, a shoebox of business cards was quietly added to throughout the year, in preparation for the following Contacts Day. At last, as Donata said in her interview for *La Nazione* in 1987, here was a holiday where the cards themselves would keep on giving, each and every year. She also joined Fabiola as a part-owner of her stationery shop, earning money from each year's fresh orders for cards.

The inevitable, however, occurred in spring 1988, when household shoeboxes were suddenly raided. The culprits: children, stirred into a frenzy by a new craze to collect the city.

Soon, stockbrokers' private lines were exchanged in the playground for the fax numbers of academics. Games of Pairs were played with the city's business community. Cards with gold lettering were worth two made from cheap white card stock. Unique designs meant scarcity—and scarcity was everything to the grubby fingers in the schoolyard.

Parents were at first amused, then outraged as they realised that they had been traded by their own children, along with their friends and neighbors, in exchange for a plumber with an attractive pipe design as a border.

At first, teachers tried to reason with the children, running special lessons on the importance of secret information and social networks. But to no avail. The most valuable card in all the playground remained that of Gil, the old TV repairman, because he had made his in the shape of a television *and* had died the previous year. Only two children had Gil, and they had obtained him only through acrimonious bidding wars involving school lunches and homework.

Meanwhile, exclusive information became commonplace. The mayor himself had his private number exchanged through a dozen sticky fingers, near-worthless for being nothing more than slightly embossed and in black.

Previously secret details were now in the pockets of the city's smallest citizens, emptied out by mothers on washing day—which meant that any useful contacts were carefully copied into notebooks for potential future use. The volume of playground circulation far outweighed that of Contacts Day itself, and the uniqueness of the event swiftly disappeared as the address books of parents grew fat all year round.

By 1989, it was over. The children had moved on to glittered stickers, and Contacts Day was no longer celebrated in the city. Donata sold her share of the shop back to Fabiola for exactly what she had paid for it—plus a box of 250 commemorative business cards of her own that read "Donata: Inventor of festivals and celebrations." She embarked on a career in transport, where she still works, and rarely thinks of those strange few years two decades ago.

This morning, during her day job as a ticket inspector on the railways, she has just had her first idea since that fateful day. She is on her way home right now, to sit behind this wall and sketch out the details. She is laughing, confident that this is another winner, bigger by far than Contacts Day.

Her idea is a machine that sells disposable shoes. The design in her head is almost finished, nearly perfect. All she needs now is to find the exact moment in which it belongs.

ViA di SANTO SPirito, 49

When she opened the envelope, she knew it wasn't him. She picked up the small, tightly sealed plastic bag, shook it a little, and looked away, holding it in one hand, weighing it gently. She gazed into it, at the reflections of her kitchen strip lights. She pressed her nose against it. It smelled of plastic.

She moved it from hand to hand. The contents of the bag looked like a diet plan milkshake. It didn't look like seventy-six years (or so he had said) of a life.

She pressed it against her cheek, against her neck, against her bosom. It was smooth and cool. The corners of the bag were pointed, and they tickled her skin. She hadn't expected any of this. It must have been his last request, she thought, closing her eyes and seeing him again in front of her, feeling the heat from his wrinkles, smelling the sweat on his brow, giggling at the rub of the smooth tips of his trembling fingers on her arm.

She opened her eyes again. No. This wasn't him. She placed the bag back in the envelope and wrote "Return to sender" on its front.

She didn't realize that, in doing so, the tip of the pen had made the tiniest of incisions in the package, enough for a grain the size of a speck of dust to float out. As she moved the package to the table by the front door, a line of particles as thin as a convent whisper exhaled into the air.

Throughout the journey from door to post office, post office to head office, head office to van, van to train, train to van, van to post office, post office to bicycle, bicycle to letter

box, he slowly sighed through the tiny pinhead opening, marking the impossible distance between his home and hers with the finest threads of himself.

He had lived a few doors down from the Società per la Cremazione. He'd known the society president well; they'd often been found exchanging drinks and gossip in the bar on the corner and it was the president who had been entrusted with sending the package to the other end of the country. The postwoman knew nothing of this. She parked her bicycle and grabbed the last of the day's letters from her bag. She paused to lock her bicycle, squeezing the mail in her hand, forcing out a final trickle of grey invisibility that settled on an anonymous doorstep.

Ten minutes later, the society president was in turn confused, surprised, and then horrified to find that he had been sent an empty parcel.

Piazza del Duomo, 18

Pancrazio bought the building because it was number 18 on the street. Numbers are very important to Pancrazio. He has spent his life studying how they interact on every level, from molecular to galactic. Which is why he numbered the rooms in his building extremely carefully before renting them out. For the purposes of his experiment, their sum could not go into double figures, except for the flat in which he lived, and the tenants had to be the (n+1)th person to reply to the advertisement.

People, he argues, are shaped by the numbers under which they live. We are all, he says, subconsciously altered by our postal code, our door number, our birth date, and our telephone numbers. If one knows about the effect, one can observe it. And perhaps, one day, use that information to tell us about ourselves.

His flat is the neutral, control position from which he documents all of his tenants' comings and goings. When the couple at number 31 talk to the person in 44, he jots it down in his pad. When 26 began a short-lived love affair with 21, he drew a number of lines connecting the two, and he was pleased to predict the joint buying of a yacht by numbers 52 and 43. When he observed number 27 receiving a two-euro coin from a shuffling man by the front door, he predicted a death in 51's family. When 34 tripped over the lead of 25's dog in the hallway, and 52 and 27 between them helped diffuse the situation, he stayed up through the following night filling half a sketchpad with scribbled formulae and notes.

Fueled by gossip, observation, and barely forgivable invasions of privacy, Pancrazio has built up a number of charts, patterns, and algebraic theories based entirely on the movements and telephone numbers of his tenants, none of whose real names will appear in the final academic paper.

When he eventually finishes the work, which according to his calculations should be 1,378 days after he began, he plans to live alone.

via Nazionale, 16

Xiao Pei Wen is one of the most highly regarded musicians in Taiwan. She confounds her audiences with manipulated sounds so strange that in her last concert, audience members reported the following to medical staff (who are always on standby whenever she appears):

8 cases of dizziness

32 cases of temporary amnesia

34 cases of mild vertigo

2 inexplicable sensations that a "presence" was sitting on their lap and blowing in their ear

12 instances of having a sudden desire for another audience member, despite their never having met

And every single person of the assembled 1,700 could smell something best described by the music critic R. P. Yan as "slightly sweet but not," and by audience member and delivery worker Mr. C. H. Tchung as "like swallowing honey while a chili-flavored ice cube was pressed against my forehead."

Xiao Pei Wen has always denied any trickery beyond installing an extra speaker above the heads of the audience to make the sound "drip from above as well as wash from every corner." Her manager remains impassive and silent to all queries. The recorded CDs sell well, but the effect, as one would expect, is somewhat diluted. The packaging contains the warning "Do not listen while driving."

Until this year, she had never left the Far East, but, in the search for new stimuli and with the hope of escaping the paparazzi, she has embarked on a tour of European cultural centers, spending a month in each one. Her plan is to create a six-act performance, each section carrying the names of her destinations; "Paris" was in postproduction and "Amsterdam" still in outline form when she arrived at the flat in Florence that she shares with her ever-present discoverer, mentor, and producer, Chen Yee Lin.

So far, five of the main art galleries in the city have witnessed the same ritual: she stands in front of pictures or sculptures she finds "interesting to my heart of my pancreas," as she puts it in her only English-language interview to date. Chen Yee Lin stands attentive, notepad in hand. Xiao Pei Wen closes her eyes and hums a note, barely louder than a whisper. When he is sure that he has heard its exact pitch and quiver, Chen Yee Lin lets out a flat, toneless bark of "MmmmaaAAAA." Then she hums again. The next note is louder; it is met with the same response from Chen Yee Lin. The next hum is louder still, shorter this time, until they create together a fast crescendo of singing and barking. After a minute or so (sometimes less), she opens her eyes, smiles, glances over his notes, always nods (she never makes a comment or suggestion), and moves on to the next exhibit. The notes will be translated back into sound by Chen Yee Lin during long hours in a recording studio at the next location.

Sometimes tourists take photos of her in action. She sighs each time, wishes she could escape her fame, but in fact they just find her amusing, and none of them know who she is.

VIA ROMANA, 5

No-one enjoys working for Maximillian. He scowls. He glowers. He shakes his head slowly and tightens his lips so thin that they look like dried spaghetti. It doesn't matter what is handed to the Direttore of the Banco di Roccia—an espresso, a birthday card, an unusual political conundrum. He will always reply with the same silent stare.

"I don't know what happened to him," whispered Maria, the office manager, to Giovanni on his first day at work, "but it turned his face to stone."

A few days after he'd started his new job, Giovanni's young family decided to surprise him at the office. His wife and four children surrounded his desk. Giovanni happily showed them around the small space, carefully avoiding Maximillian's private office.

The Direttore himself was reading through a list of numbers, which related somehow to more numbers on other sheets of paper. He picked up a book from the far edge of the desk, glanced down, and found his gaze met by the clear blue eyes of Giovanni's four-year-old son.

The boy stared up at Maximillian. The middle-aged man said nothing. He frowned at the child. Then he grimaced. His body didn't move. His eyes slowly crossed, his forehead folded in on itself, and his cheeks clenched together to press tight against his nose. His mouth creaked into an uneven grin, his tongue waggled, and, buried somewhere inside the pink folds of what no longer looked much like a face, two pinhole eyes twinkled.

The child squealed and laughed, rolled on the floor, and tried to use fingers and thumbs to press his features into anything as gruesomely delightful.

Maximillian twitched his ears as a coup de grace and then slowly unfolded his face with the elegance and ease of an expensive cabriolet gently tucking away its automatic roof. With a wink, he then looked back down at the numbers in his hand.

The boy ran out of the room giggling, straight into his father who looked in horror at where his errant offspring had been. Maximillian glanced up and grunted as Giovanni apologized profusely and quietly closed the office door.

Over the following week, everything continued as before. But Maximillian's facial origami had been spotted by Maria, from her desk across the office. A few days later, she decided to test something. She borrowed her five-year-old niece on an afternoon when she knew that the monthly reports would put Maximillian in an even worse mood than normal. Maria pretended not to watch as the small girl pushed open his door, handed him the report as Maria had told her to, and was answered not in words but with a rolling of the eyeballs and a broad flexing of the Direttore's nostrils. She ran back to her aunt in a giggling fit.

A rotation now exists, listing all small children—neighbours', relatives', friends'—who can be borrowed when needed. Any budget requests, and all other unfavorable reports, sent to the Banco di Roccia of Florence are now delivered to the head of the operation by a succession of miniature messengers, who leave giggling and pulling hideous faces at their parents for the rest of the day.

It doesn't seem to improve the mood of the Direttore himself. It doesn't improve his behavior in the office. But at least, on days when they know that the news is bad, his staff can gather around Maria's desk and have something to look forward to.

No one knows what happened here.

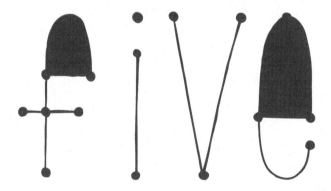

Borgo Santi Apostoli, 25

It isn't the most obvious slogan for their group.

"It translates from the Latin as 'skill and trustworthiness,'" says Dino.

"But what does that have to do with us?" asks Giacomo, who doesn't know that his name is usually said to mean "The Supplanter."

"No, no, Dino has a point," says Isabella ("Consecrated to God") firmly, staring into Dino's eyes in that way that always unnerves him. "Skill and trustworthiness. It's what everything's about. I like it."

"As the official Deputy President (acting) of The Spokespeople for Buskers, Artists Who Make Things Out of Wire* (*except human figures), Soft Drink Can Ashtray Makers, and Assorted Performers of No Fixed Pavement, I would question our need for a motto at all," says Fiorello ("Little Flower"). "But we will of course put it to a vote."

So they do, following which Rocio—"Dewdrops," she once discovered to her distaste—loudly announces that the motion has been denied. The group, who live in an impossibly cheap set of rooms on the undemolished side of a building overlooking the train tracks, must remain temporarily without a slogan.

"Erm, except, erm, we already have a bell."

Dino holds it up, sheepishly. "I found it in a dumpster. I don't know who had it before. But I thought it would suit."

Ugo, "Bright in Mind and Spirit," and Verdi, "Green," call an immediate huddle. Dino sits apart from it, his cheeks red with embarrassment.

"We've changed our minds," beams Neroli ("Orange Blossom").

Dino—who was told five years ago that his name meant "Little Sword"—will wire it up himself that afternoon.

BORGO 12 OGNISSANTI,

The dancers arrive every Monday. This week, there are four Spaniards staying there, touring with a flamenco show. Last week, there were a sixty-year-old man and a twenty-year-old woman who was but four feet tall. They all practice on the sprung floor in the flat and sleep on the mattresses piled up against the far wall. Each week brings a change in music, style, people, purpose . . . but it's always dancers.

Keith doesn't mind the music, but he wishes they wouldn't smoke on the balcony. For it is the smoke and not the dancers that floats through his open kitchen window.

Borgo La Noce, Thirty - Eight

Ali Jamalzadeh is not deaf, but he pretends to be. He's an ex-professor of linguistics and an accomplished semiotician, and in his paper "The Search for International Modes of Communication: History and Future" (1987), he argued that the invented language of Esperanto, created to bring unity to the world, fails because of its inherent uselessness. "It has no good reason to exist, except as a linguistic no-man's land, a neutral space into which virtually no one can be bothered to venture," he declared, to the muttered disapproval of his colleagues. "Mankind does not gain," he concluded, "by its existence."

What Ali Jamalzadeh didn't add was that he had a plan, a blueprint for how to improve society through the creation of a new language. Four years after delivering that paper, he retired to Florence in order to dedicate the rest of his life to the mission. And so he is currently halfway through the first-ever dictionary of Sordish, the international sign language for everyone.

It started as a theory. If a sign language were to be adopted by hearing society, reasoned Professor Emeritus Ali Jamalzadeh, it would immediately enfranchise a previously excluded section of the population. Plus there were innumerable advantages to being able to communicate without resorting to the fickle fortunes of sound waves—across a crowded room, during a church service, at a particularly loud rock concert.

Professor Jamalzadeh has dedicated the previous decade and a half to becoming the world's only fluent communicator in twelve sign languages. (He can also get by in eight others.) He writes poetry in them. He has even written a collection of silent, multilingual signed songs. His only spoken languages are English and Italian; however, almost no one in his adopted city knows that he can speak at all.

He uses his voice only a few times a week, to run innocent-sounding classes on writing and linguistics inside schools and prisons—while covertly teaching his new creation to the students. His reasoning is that once this crowd understands its usefulness, Sordish will immediately become essential knowledge also for the supervisors of the children and criminals. And thus the language will grow and spread. By slowly turning it into a societal necessity, he hopes Sordish will be the key to the lock that Esperanto has failed to pick.

But all of that is for later. For now, Ali Jamalzadeh continues to pretend that he is deaf, so that he can immediately address the creation of a new vocabulary that is useful in everyday life. He estimates that the *Dictionary of Sordish* (First Edition) is probably about three-quarters written. But there are always more words to uncover.

So, when you press this doorbell, a light flashes in the flat. It's an expensive detail, and not a strictly necessary one. However, in case of unexpected guests, he feels it important to keep up appearances.

LUNGARNO AMERIGO VESPUCCI, 27

As soon as Giovanni gets here, they'll start to play. After all, what would "Arabela ed i Cowboys" be without Arabela? She said enough was enough, but she'd said it before and they'd never believed her. However angry she'd felt, she had always turned up for the gigs, sulking on arrival but smiling and laughing with them again by the start of the first chorus.

She always turned up for the gigs. Except this time. This time, the Easter festival crowd is still waiting for them to play, but they aren't on stage yet because Arabela isn't there. Gerodi, Benni, and Filippi left Giovanni back at the venue as they rushed to her house, rang her doorbell, pleaded with her through the tinny speaker, all the while staring at the tiny camera through which they knew she was watching them.

"Just one farewell gig," Filippi begged.

"Play it without me," she said, and hung up.

So that's what they'll do. One swift phone call later and it was decided. As soon as Giovanni arrives with the instruments, they'll set themselves up on the pavement, ring the doorbell, wait until they know she's watching on the tiny monochrome screen in her flat, and play that farewell concert squarely at her front door.

If she doesn't join in over the speakerphone by the start of the first chorus, then they'll know it's time to change the name of the band.

VIA DELL'
ARIENTO,
●●● ●●●●

"Fate is a bastard."
—*trad. Florentine saying, thirteenth century*

THIRTY

The money kept coming. No matter how much Felice protested, the money kept coming. Even though his year was up, his grant had ended, the city councilors had assured him more than once that it would not be renewed, and then subsequently denied that it was happening, a significant sum was still being placed in his account, without fail, on the third of every month.

The only question was what to do with it. He had already let go of his research staff. He had enough from his inheritance to survive without the substantial grant; frivolous spending wasn't his style, plus, if this stipend came from the city, he felt he should spend it in a socially responsible way. But how?

He was pondering this problem, sitting at the foot of the Cosimo I de' Medici statue in Piazza della Signoria, when someone tapped him on the shoulder.

"You won't believe this," said the girl standing above him, "but I think this is your umbrella."

He stared at the object she was holding and knew it to be true. A month earlier, he had accidentally left the umbrella in a small café in Prato, a small town he had visited with a friend on the sole basis that they thought it had a funny name. The girl now standing in front of him had been their waitress, and he and she had flirted shamelessly, which had made her blush and then miscalculate the bill in their favour.

"And I believe," replied Felice with gallant nonchalance, "that I owe your establishment the cost of two beers and a slice of cake. May I have the honour of purchasing them now?"

Later that evening, and a few more than two beers later, they leaned on each other to correct the rotation of the earth and gazed at the dark reflections that were drifting down the river. She sighed happily and gave a tiny hiccup.

"Who'd have thought, of all the places and all the times, that I'd come to Florence today, with your umbrella in case it rained, and sit by that statue right then? We couldn't have arranged it better."

Felice agreed absently, letting the glare from a nearby second-floor window stain his blurry retina. Then he blinked and turned to face her. "Say that again," he said, swaying a little at the bolt of sobriety that had just struck his brain.

"Err . . . who'd have thought we'd be here right now?"

"No, the other bit."

"That . . . that we couldn't have made this happen even if we'd wanted to?"

"Exactly." He grinned, showing all his teeth, right up to the molars. "Exactly! But I bet we could."

Six months later, Felice cleared his throat and looked at the seven happy faces sitting around the table. This was the first meeting held in the group's second studio space. Things were expanding fast, yet again there were new people at the table, even more boxes were piled up in the corridor, and the throb of fresh paint was making them all a little giddy.

"So, what have you got?"

Eufemia, the girl with the umbrella, looked up at her lover and smiled. "Well . . . I have news. I've found that a woman called Arabela, who was the childhood friend of Fidelio Mazereni, lives four blocks away from him and he doesn't seem to know it."

Felice flashed his molars at her. "And the plan?"

"Me and Brunilda have been following them closely. Arabela is job hunting right now, and it turns out that his fruit shop is advertising for staff, so we left a message containing her details. If all goes well, he'll call her soon enough, and then they'll meet."

Felice nodded sagely. "Very good. Next?"

Maurizio raised his hand. "We're still working on Signor Attrizzi. He hasn't encountered his former doorman yet, so we've set up a situation that will make that happen."

"What kind of situation?"

"We've rented the flat on the third floor of the doorman's current workplace and are asking Signor Attrizzi to measure it for curtains. We'll cancel the order the following day, of course, and leave the place by the end of the week, once the mission is completed."

"Excellent. Anyone else?"

"Giulia and I are still in the city archives," replied a middle-aged man whose features and demeanor always reminded Felice not so much of a person as a leather-bound dictionary. "We've got four new possibilities, three confirmed 'school connections' that we're tracking, and one trio who all used to go to a church in Fiesole that no longer exists. Natanaele is working on getting all the parts that the couple on Borgo la Noce need for their plumbing work and placing them in dumpsters on their route to the grocery store, and we've put five relevant books for Leoni Carlucci's forthcoming thesis at the front of the secondhand bookshop she'll pass by tomorrow on the way to pick up her dry cleaning."

Felice nodded, scribbling a few notes in a notebook that was cryptically labeled "Earl Grey." Six months in, his secret project, Coincidences Happen, was going rather well. Until its formation, the city was as full and devoid of random encounters as fickle chance determined. Now, thanks to his dedicated group's researching, scouring for information, carefully directed small talk, and above all, waiting and watching, idle luck had a backup team.

He looked around absently, sliding his hand into his pocket to jangle his keys. His fingertips curled around something cold and round. "Good," he said absently. "Good. Do you know, a funny thing happened this morning." He pulled from his pocket a two-euro coin. "A man came up to me, smiled, and gave me this. And then walked away without a word! Funny thing."

Orazio, Nevio, and Samuela shifted uncomfortably in their seats and then produced two-euro coins of their own.

He stared at them for a moment, and then everyone began to laugh. Things like that happened all the time.

VICOLO deGLI ADIMARI, 5

Everyone was on holiday when Dr Segrini arrived. Nobody saw him enter the building. No one was around when the van brought his things. He moved into his new rooms uninterrupted, which suited him just fine. He had had to leave his last premises in a hurry and was keen to avoid any inquiring neighbours.

So it was last week, when Signor Galli, Signora Ciarletta, Signor Minghetti, and the rest returned from their respective holidays to find old Signora Partencia's flat occupied, and a new name on the bell.

"Did you see?" Signora Bernadetta Ciarletta asks Dr. Ulisse Gloriati in a hushed tone on the stairwell.

"See what?" he replies, frowning.

"The new 'Doctor,'" she says, with a mocking tip of the head.

"I've seen nothing," he says.

"On your way out, take a look at the bell," she says, with a knowing smile. "You'll see."

Dr. Gloriati returns her leer with a small, confused grin and walks down the remaining flight of stairs. He carefully closes the door behind him before peering up at the panel of doorbells. Segrini. It doesn't seem to bode any ill will or danger. And then he sees what she had been referring to. The name itself is normal enough, but the rectangle of metal on which it sits is significantly larger than the others. There is no rule against it, of course. But it does stand out a little.

"Is that it?" he thinks, shaking his head at the small-minded, gossip-filled existence of Signora Ciarletta.

In spare moments throughout the day, Dr. Gloriati's thoughts idly return to the metal panel. At first he thinks it ridiculous to attach such importance to tiny details. So what if the newcomer has chosen a somewhat unusual way of announcing his occupancy? Signora Ciarletta could respond with neon lights and a blaring horn, for all he cares. "What a silly woman," he says under his breath in those quiet pauses between patients.

Then, at around half-past three, between the groaning joints of a geriatric and the bellyaching of a child who is almost certainly trying to avoid a history exam, he suddenly asks himself why the new doctor, whose name means nothing to him, has chosen such a method of presentation. Is he, perhaps, making some kind of statement about his status? Will he indeed become an important figure on the street? Will prominent visitors be seeking him out? Is this the reason for his deliberate act of self-aggrandizement?

Or, he thinks with a jolt, as his cold stethoscope presses against the gurgling stomach of an eight-year-old, what if this message isn't intended for visitors at all? What if it is a subtle attack on the only other doctor in the flat block?

His own name has been displayed there for three years, and he has occasionally permitted himself a tiny glow of pride when glancing over the names on the bells, satisfied with his educated status compared to those around him. That feeling is gone now, of course. A layman standing by the door glancing over the bells will see nothing but a group of average people surrounded by two—not one, but two—doctors.

And which of those doctors will appear, to the uneducated eye, to have the higher status? Why, the larger-signposted of the two, naturally. The so-called Dr Segrini.

Many of his own clients are people he sees socially. What will they think as they stand in front of the lintel, casually looking over the names as they await his descent? He is, in their eyes at least, a man of high regard. Yet now he seems no longer the most important doctor in his own building.

Now he remembers Signora Ciarletta's words, her mocking gesture when she had said the word "Doctor." He had assumed it was directed at the new occupant. What if it had been meant for him? Was she in fact suggesting that his status had now changed, is no longer that of a well-respected gentleman in the building?

After so long, and such struggle for the recognition, had he been so swiftly replaced? What else did she know about the new arrival?

"Is there a problem?" asks the boy's mother, her face pale as she tracks each of Dr. Gloriati's tiny facial twitches, his stethoscope still pressing against her son's pale belly.

"Hm? Oh. No. It's fine. He'll be fine," he replies, removing the earpieces and dismissing both the woman and her snotty son with a wave of his hand.

There is no question about it. He will have to confront the aggressive new Doctor this evening, before the whole thing gets out of hand. Perhaps it is a mere misunderstanding, a creation of his imagination. Perhaps the new Doctor will welcome him in, laugh at such irrelevances over a shared brandy, curse an inept engraver, and then change the bell the following day without a second thought. Perhaps.

Four hours later, Dr. Gloriati approaches the door of Dr. Segrini's flat. He hammers on its dark wood panels in what he hopes is a firm yet unthreatening manner. He is wearing his leather gloves and has buttoned up his coat to give an air of authority. He will remove the coat if the welcome is warm; he will keep it on if the tone is frosty. But there is no answer.

He bends onto one knee and peers through the keyhole. The lights are off, and he can see nothing but a white wall in the gloom behind the door. Hasn't this man even furnished his house yet?

Dr Gloriati retreats to his own flat. He closes the door behind him and, without removing his overcoat, sits in his armchair and closes his eyes. Not for the first time that day, he is replaying in his head some of the conflict that may soon occur. He silently mouths his steely, polite greetings, imagining one reply, then another, priming his responses to all eventualities. Before too long, the issue will be resolved, and he will have his way.

The next day, Dr. Gloriati spends those empty, quiet moments in his surgery preparing increasingly aggressive replies to the casual dismissals and angry sideswipes that he is beginning to expect from his potential new nemesis. This is to be a game of chess, a fencing match, a pure battle of wits. The first move has been made, in full view of the world no less, on the wall outside their shared front door. Soon it will be time for his riposte.

It is now 2:34 in the afternoon. Dr. Gloriati is attending to an elderly gentleman with flatulence. Meanwhile, near to where he lives, a short woman in sunglasses and a smart poncho is standing on the corner. She calls out loudly to a passerby.

"Excuse me, can you direct me to the door of Vicolo degli Adimari, number 5?"

The pedestrian points at a nearby doorway, starts to move away, then looks at the woman, who hasn't moved. He goes back, realizes his error, and then takes her arm in his. They walk the short distance together in silence. He announces their arrival in a loud voice.

"Thank you so much," she says and then, as she did many times before at his previous address, reaches up at the wall to feel for Dr. Segrini's bell.

VIA MAFFIA, 36

Neither Signor nor Signora Neppi suspected anything. He's lived there for every one of his fifty-four years, and his family has occupied the building for at least seven generations. In that time, the house has been inside as it appears from the outside: a reasonably smart two-story residence, built around the late 1600s, divided by solid interior walls into several decent-sized rooms.

It would be the perfect home for a large family of a certain social status; the Neppis are both childless and impecunious, and their meager income combined with their savings barely covers the property tax. But Signor Neppi cannot bear the thought of leasing out any room that still bears the shadows of his happy and luxurious childhood, even less of moving to somewhere of a more suitable size. All but four of the rooms have remained closed to save on heating, in the hope that something would turn up to resolve the issue.

A few months ago, something did turn up—or rather, down. Signor Neppi was in the kitchen on the ground floor when he pulled his handkerchief from his pocket, accidentally tugging with it a two-euro coin. It dropped, edge down, straight through a crack in the floorboards.

He was so distracted by his clumsiness, he failed to hear a distant thud a few seconds later. He reached into the cupboard under the sink for his tool kit and began to work on lifting the floorboards. His wife watched with the idle curiosity of one enjoying an unexpected change of routine.

On lifting the first floorboard, he yelled a word she had never heard him say. Where the heavy strip of timber had been was a dark hole. She passed him a flashlight from his toolbox and together they peered down. Far beneath them seemed to be a large room, empty except for dust. "Over there, there's something over there," cried Signora Neppi as the light passed over the far corners. He moved the flashlight to where she was pointing. It was a doorway.

An hour later, Signor Neppi had raised two more floor-boards. He had changed his clothes into ones he didn't mind getting dusty and was about to climb down a tall ladder that he had lowered through the hole. "You stay up here, dear," he said, a twitch of fear spoiling the left side of his confident smile. "And if, you know, I fall or something, then go next door and get Guillermo and Anna. Don't try to follow me."

He began to climb down. After a few seconds, his head reemerged through the hole. "I do love you, Chiara," he said, and again started his descent. It was the first time this year he had said it.

He waved up at his wife's anxious face, then focused the flashlight on the dusty room he was about to step into. The walls were gray, the floor solid, containing nothing but dust and the detritus of generations of fallen crumbs. And there, to one side, was his two-euro coin. He stepped off the ladder onto the solid floor, reached down and pocketed the coin.

Signor Neppi pulled out his handkerchief and held it over his mouth as he tentatively stepped forward to the empty doorway. All was dark and silent. The flashlight revealed a dark corridor made of brick, with more doorways beyond.

Signor Neppi was astonished at the enormity of it all . . . and yet something seemed oddly familiar.

Behind him, there was a slow scraping sound followed by a whoosh and a loud crash. Something had brushed past his shoulder. He spun around and saw only an enormous cloud of dust heading straight for him. He closed his eyes and held his breath as it ran into and through him. He heard his wife scream.

He waited. He counted to five, feeling the last of the dust clouds settle over his face. All was silent. He had never felt so alone. "Are you OK?" he shouted through the handkerchief.

Silence. Then he heard a tiny voice. "I'm . . . I'm so sorry Costanzo. I was leaning in, I nudged it . . . it just slipped."

He opened his eyes carefully and saw the ladder flat on the floor at his feet. "No harm done, dear," he said, relieved. "I'll just raise it up again." Then he saw the damage: the left side of the ladder had splintered in two by the impact of its fall.

"Go next door, ask them for a ladder," he shouted up to her. "Don't worry about me. Don't worry, it's fine." She nodded, and her face disappeared from the hole in the ceiling.

He sighed and turned back to the dark doorway. He knew something about this space, something that was familiar and yet strange. What could it be? And what was it doing underneath his house?

He stepped into the dark corridor and walked through a brick archway. Another empty room. He stepped back to the corridor, unnerved. The next doorway led to a further room, empty too. He walked into this space, through another doorway at the far end, and then suddenly stopped. He shone his flashlight onto the right-hand wall and saw exactly what he had somehow expected: a staircase, leading down.

Two days later, with Guillermo's help, he had rigged a series of lights along the corridors, and his wife was about to make her first descent down the steel ladder that Signor Neppi had purchased after that surprising first day. He waited for her by the bottom rung. Her arms shook as she took each step carefully, looking down not at the floor but at the patient, smiling face of her husband.

She gripped his hand and took the final step onto the floor, her flat shoe slipping slightly on the dust. He grinned as she looked around uncertainly.

"You already know your way around," he said.

It was just as he had promised—an exact mirror image of the house above, each room in the same place as its above-ground equivalent. Where steps went up in the daylight world, they went down here—both stories represented in exact detail, every room as empty as if it had just been built. Except, where the stairs above ground ended at the second story, here they went down two levels more, to two reasonable-sized rooms, and then finally some tiny stairs led to a final, small basement.

Each room was completely empty, except the final attic/basement, where Signor Neppi found, on a small wooden stool, a handwritten ledger labeled "NEPPI 1683." It contained only numbers, in neat columns, and was incomplete.

Now, three and a half months later, the plans have been agreed to and construction has begun. In the initial plans, he numbered the rooms on each level in the traditional manner, but the problems of underground housing, together with the need for additional plumbing, meant that some of the first rooms soon were taken up with water tanks, electricity cables, and such. Signora Neppi is overseeing the creation of each small basement flat, a task she is enjoying greatly.

After a long discussion, it was also decided that the final two stories would remain closed. There's something about them that made Signora Neppi feel uneasy, and in any case, they have enough money from the bank only for this first phase. The rooms are too dark for most Italians, and so they have decided that their target will be American college students. The doorbell, with their name written in English at the top, was installed three days ago. Within a month, they hope to advertise the underground rooms as available for rent.

Signor Neppi still can't bear the idea of getting lodgers for the rooms he and his family played in when he was a child. But the mirror house, strange as it is, holds no memories for him of any kind. He is currently searching his family tree for wealthy seventeenth-century eccentrics, so that they know whom to thank.

Via Romana

She knows he can't be there, but that's OK. He's traveling, and anyway it's just a silly ceremony. Hairdressing college is hardly the University of Padua, and she'll see him very soon, so it doesn't really matter so much.

She's standing there now, alongside her classmates, smiling at the front of the rented hall, thinking of her future and thinking of him. Meanwhile, back at her house, an electrician is standing, looking at the wall, smiling also. The bell is well made and easy to fit into place. And the young gentleman had tipped him extremely well to fit it at this particular hour on this particular day.

He takes his cloth, gives it a final polish, and slips his card through the letterbox. He then copies down the address of the client on a scrap of paper. A bell like this must mean a very skilled and successful hairdresser. He will tell his wife, who will probably come the very next morning to try it out.

Eight

via dell Ariento 37

After twelve years, they decided to let Mario Rossi go. His body had recovered as much as it was going to; he could walk now, albeit with a shuffle that made him look much older than he was. He still refused to speak, he still had somewhat strange habits, and, when pushed to communicate with a pen and paper, he still claimed complete amnesia about his life before the accident. But he was harmless, there had been cutbacks, and his bed was now needed for someone else.

He was handed a large brown envelope containing his possessions. He looked at them with interest. Nothing seemed familiar, but it all seemed intriguing. A bank book. A letter from an insurance company, care of the hospital, confirming a substantial payout. Papers from a lawyer, confirming that all issues of tax and administration were being taken care of using a fraction of the money in his account. A letter confirming a state pension for invalids. A wallet containing three thousand lire, an ID card and the business card of a bar. A set of house keys.

The hospital called a taxi, gave the driver the address written in his bank book, and gave him money for the journey. Mario waved genially at his now former hosts as he was driven away.

"This is the place," said the driver. Mario shrugged. It seemed as likely as anywhere. They both got out of the car. The fare came to two euros less than the amount the hospital had given him, and so the driver gave him a two-euro coin as his change. Mario looked at this strange new money, then handed it back. The driver's face widened with pleasure and surprise. "Thank you very much signor, very kind," he said. He then made a show of lifting Mario's suitcase onto the front step for him before getting back into his cab and driving away.

Mario stood on the doorstep, suitcase at his side, and looked around. None of it reminded him of anything. He tried one of the keys in the lock. It fit.

After a week of dusting and cleaning, the flat had become habitable again. Three weeks after that, Mario sat in his flat and watched people from his window. Although nothing was familiar from before the accident, he had established something of a routine: he would wake around 8 A.M., shower, get dressed, then shuffle his way through the streets to the park. He would sit there a while, then head back to the flat via the shops. He made himself lunch—it seemed that he was a reasonable cook—and then spent an hour or so looking with detached interest at some of the objects filling the boxes and drawers of the flat. Then he would return to his seat by the window, watch the streets again until he was tired, and then he would go to bed.

So far, he had found plenty of books in the flat, as well as clothes that seemed to be his, a large collection of old schoolbooks, and dictionaries of First Names, Plants and Flowers, Etymology, and Spanish (a language of which he had no memory whatsoever). He had, it seemed, worked in the local library, but he felt no inclination to return. After all, twelve years had passed, and he knew nothing of the work that would be expected of him. He was also worried that the same thing would happen that had occurred in the bar whose card he'd found in his wallet. He had headed that way with much expectation and excitement, feeling sure that here at last would be a clue to his former life—only to find it had been converted into a dress shop several years earlier.

The strange thing about everything in his flat was that there was absolutely no record of any friends or family. He was, he supposed, both a learned and a lonely person. There were no photographs anywhere, no letters received or personal gifts dedicated to him. The only thing he found, at the bottom of his underwear drawer, was a small white card that said, "With love, G." It had obviously been important enough to hold onto, so he determined to keep doing so, even though he had no idea why.

As Mario shuffled his way through the streets, he found himself staring into the faces of everyone he passed, looking for someone or something he might recognize. He soon realised that people found this unnerving, and so he mastered the art of staring at them from a distance, or out of the corner of his eye. He didn't know what he was looking for, but he would know it when he saw it. And then, one day, there it was—a particular kind of melancholy, a deep sigh from behind the eyes that saw the world as something to be wary of.

He didn't know why, but he knew that look; he knew it very well. He grabbed the hand of the young man who wore it, a young man who happened to be serving him in a butcher's shop. Mario pointed gleefully at himself, hoping for some recognition between the two of them. But the boy just snatched his hand away and said, "Are you gay or something?" in an aggressive way that made Mario think he had been mistaken.

A few days later, while shaving, Mario realised why he had recognized that empty look so clearly. It was the look of his reflection in the mirror. He remembered back to the taxi ride from the hospital, and the surprised, delighted response from the driver's face when Mario had given him that coin. It had transformed the man's face, and had made him look so happy, so alive. He continued to stare at himself in the mirror. He wanted to see the driver's expression again, this time on a different face, on every face he came across that held that aching loneliness that would not otherwise go away.

Later that day, he went to the bank carrying a small suitcase on wheels that he had found at the back of a closet. He handed his bank book over to the teller, along with a small piece of paper asking for all his insurance money to be converted into two-euro coins. He was told that there was a daily limit, that they did not have that many coins in the branch. He waved a hand at the suitcase. Whatever they had, whatever could fit inside. They understood.

The next day, his shuffling was slower than usual, weighed down by the bags of coins in his pockets. He wasn't sure why he carried them, but felt certain that something would come up.

He sat on a bench in the middle of the park, and waited. Within ten minutes, three dogs and their walker stopped close by. The woman holding the leashes yawned and looked down at the ground as she allowed her pets to tug and sniff around a tree, straining her shoulder blades with their keen exploration.

Mario tapped her on the shoulder, smiled, and placed one of the two-euro coins in her hand. "What's this for?" she demanded. He shrugged, smiled again, and began to shuffle away. "Why are you giving me this?" she called after him. He continued his walk, and then turned and saw a confused smile on her face. For a moment, the world neither made sense, nor was against her. The sigh had gone from behind her eyes. And she looked right at him in surprised gratitude. So this was it. This was the meaning his life had lacked. He would find people who needed the elevating powers of a small, bimetallic coin and allow them a moment of freedom from the ordered world that was holding them back.

Over the following five months, he gave away a total of €1,148 in two-euro coins. Sometimes he'd go back to the same person again and again. Mostly, though, they were all different people, people with a sadness that he couldn't help but see. He could never be sure he hadn't known them before, but he hoped that they would remember him fondly either way.

However, after a while it became repetitive, even for him. It had been in some way helpful, and he still had plenty of coins piled up on his dining table, but he soon realised that there were too many, it was all too much. He now saw the sadness everywhere he looked, he didn't know where to begin anymore. He needed another idea.

One day, not too long ago, he paused on his own front step and looked across at the doorbell. Something was different. The names inside the plastic had all been rewritten in a very neat hand. He wondered who had done this, and why he or she had taken offense at what was there before. He began to dream a story in his head, about an unemployed graphologist who was over-sensitive to handwriting. It made him smile.

He shuffled down the street, his head now buzzing with ideas. He turned the corner, and a yellow piece of paper caught his eye. He slowly approached it and saw that the doorbell at this particular house didn't work. Perhaps, he thought, the voice inside was too beautiful to bear listening to.

This is how it began.

Mario Rossi now spends his days looking at doorbells. Each day he dreams up people he doesn't know from the names he sees, creating a whole new Florence in his mind—a Florence as strange and laughable as a short shuffling man with no memory and a pile of two-euro coins on his dining table.

If you happen to see him, slowly making his way along the streets of Florence, say hello from me. He gave me two euros once, without a word, and I'll never forget him.